D1241271

# ZOOMAN AND THE SIGN

**by Charles Fuller**

NELSON DOUBLEDAY, INC.
*Garden City, New York*

*Zooman and the Sign* opened on December 7, 1980 at Theatre Four in New York City. It was presented by the Negro Ensemble Company, Gerald S. Krone Managing Director, Douglas Turner Ward Artistic Director. Direction was by Douglas Turner Ward; scenery by Rodney J. Lucas; lighting by Shirley Pendergast; and costumes by Judy Dearing. The cast, in order of appearance, was as follows:

| | |
|---|---|
| ZOOMAN | *Giancarlo Esposito* |
| RACHEL TATE | *Mary Alice* |
| EMMETT TATE | *Carl Gordon* |
| REUBEN TATE | *Ray Aranha* |
| VICTOR TATE | *Alvin Alexis* |
| RUSSELL ODOMS | *Terrance Terry Ellis* |
| DONALD JACKSON | *Steven A. Jones* |
| ASH BOSWELL | *Frances Foster* |
| GRACE GEORGES | *Carol Lynn Maillard* |

# ZOOMAN AND THE SIGN

*Characters*

REUBEN TATE
RACHEL TATE
VICTOR TATE
EMMETT TATE
ASH BOSWELL
DONALD JACKSON
RUSSELL ODOMS
GRACE GEORGES
&
ZOOMAN

Time:   The Present

Place:   Philadelphia, Pennsylvania
The home of Rachel and Reuben Tate—
The Street outside
Various locations for Zooman

# ACT ONE

# ACT I

A living room, middle class and fairly modern, though a bit or-
nate, occupies much of the stage. In the living room, the furniture is comfortable. Beyond the living room upstage right is the
front door, which leads out to a porch. The porch door opens
onto a single stoop and the sidewalk, which operates downstage, across the entire stage front. Downstage right is a
medium-sized raised platform on which an actor should be
able to pace. A staircase upstage left inside an archway corridor
leads to the second floor and to the right of the living room.
Upstage of the archway leads to an unseen dining room and
kitchen offstage.

The light rises slowly over the platform. In the spotlight standing on the platform is a young black man. He steps forward,
looking at the audience rather contemptuously. He is wearing a
mesh and plastic, green and white baseball cap tilted to the
side. A red T-shirt, with the inscription "ME" on it, hangs outside a pair of slacks or dungarees designed with two large
pockets, one on each side of the pants. He is wearing high-top
sneaks. There are several thin gold and silver chains around his
neck. He is Zooman and is always accompanied when he enters

3

*by a low, rather dissonant disco sound. As he stands looking at the audience, his music fades slightly, but lingers in the background. Zooman may carry a radio, but it is not necessary.*

ZOOMAN: Once upon a time, while the goose was drinkin' wine ole monkey robbed the people on the trolley car line. (*Laughs*) I carry a gun and a knife. A gun in this pocket—and ole "Magic" in this one! (*He removes a ten-inch switchblade knife*) Now you see it—(*Makes a stabbing gesture*) Now you don't! (*Smiles*) I cut a mothafucka with this baby yesterday. Ole foreign mothafucka walkin' on the subway platform. (*He waddles, amused*) Arms swingin' all ova everywhere—bumpin' into people—glasses, two, three inches thick standin' out from his eyes, can't half see! And I'm tryin' to listen to my music too? No-talkin' mothafucka needed to get cut. (*Smiles*) "Magic" knicked him. "Magic" is sharp as a razor. He ain't even know he was cut till he was halfway down the platform, and the blood started runnin' down the ole punk's hand. (*Looks at knife*) Mothafucka started screamin'—dropped his newspapa—jumpin' up and down, pleadin' to everybody waitin' on the subway—Ain't nobody do nothin'—ole jive West Indian mothafucka damn near got hit by a train! (*Laughs*) Fell all down on the ground and shit—peed on hisself! Shiiit, he wasn't hurt that bad! "Magic" only knicked the scared mothafucka! (*To himself after pause*) Mothafucka don't know what scared is! (*Distinct change of mood*) They call me, Zoo-man! That's right. Z-O-O-M-A-N! From the Bottom! I'm the "runner" down thea. When I knuck with a dude, I fight like a panther. Strike like a cobra! Stomp on mothafuckas like a whole herd of bi-son! Zooman! (*Irritated*) That ole mothafucka yesterday coulda put somebody's eye out. Swingin' his arms around like he owned the whole fuckin' platform. Lotta ole people take advantage of you jes' cause they old. Movin' all slow and shit—mumblin' unda they breath—shufflin' down the street all bent over and twisted up—skin hangin' all off they faces—makes my stomach turn jes' to look at 'em! I got an aunt like that. Me and Kenny useta stay to that mean bitch's house sometimes. Evil ole skunk walkin' down the avenue, one

4

mile an hour and shit, useta hit us across the mouth with a fly swatter jes' for talkin' at the mothafuckin' table! I was glad when the "junkies" would steal her check. We useta tell her, she was dumb for goin' down there—don't nobody with any sense walk on the Avenue with a social security check in they hands! (*To himself*) Lotta times we'd be to that bitch's house, three—four days, wouldn't eat nothin'. (*Casually*) What am I doing here now? I just killed somebody. Little girl, I think. Me and Stockholm turned the corner of this street?—and there's Gustav and them jive mothafuckas from uptown, and this little bitch has to be sittin' on her front steps playin' jacks—or some ole kid shit! But I had tol' Gustav if I eva saw his ass around the Avenue, I'd blow him away. (*Shrugs*) So I started shootin' and she jes' got hit by one of the strays, that's all. She ain't had no business bein' out there. That street is a war zone—ain't nobody see her, we was runnin'—shit! And in that neighborhood you supposed to stay indoors, anyway! (*Pause*) She was in the wrong place at the wrong time—how am I supposed to feel guilty over somethin' like that? Shiiit, I don't know the little bitch, anyway.

(*The lights begin to fade around Zooman as his music comes up softly in the background. Simultaneously, the light builds in the Tate living room. There the mood is heavy. Action is continuous. On the sofa Reuben Tate, a black man, sits beside his wife, Rachel, an attractive black woman. Reuben is dressed in a bus driver's uniform, Rachel in skirt, and blouse. Uncle Emmett, a man not much older than Reuben, is standing. Also there is Victor, the Tates' fifteen-year-old son. He is dressed surprisingly similarly to Zooman. Reuben attempts to comfort Rachel*)

RACHEL: I keep seeing her, Reuben—feeling her all over the room. And I want to say something to her—reach out and straighten her hair, touch her dress. And I know she's gone—

EMMETT: I say we go out there—me and you, Reub, with two pistols, hunt the little bastards down and put a goddamn bullet in each one of 'em's head! Look, these are kids that ain't *about* nothin', ain't *goin'* nowhea, and ain't *no* good—and I say let's cut our losses—I don't mind tellin' people we've got treacherous black kids out there! But let's get rid of 'em, Reub!

REUBEN: Come on, Emmett! (*To Rachel*) Try to relax, baby.

EMMETT: They just killed your daughter, nephew—on her own front steps! You think anybody's gonna look too hard for the boys who did it? Where you been? (*He is close to tears*)

REUBEN: Who do we go out and kill?

EMMETT: All of 'em with their hats tipped to the side, and them goddamn basketball sneaks on, that's who!

VICTOR: I wear sneaks, Uncle Emmett.

EMMETT: (*Quickly*) Buy you a pair of loafers then, boy!

RACHEL: (*Immediately*) Emmett, will you please stop it? You're threatening my son. Just stop it! (*There is a brief silence in the house*)

EMMETT: (*Hurt*) I'm sorry—don't pay no attention to me! Tell her, Reuben—he'll tell you, Rachel, I always say too much. I ain't gonna say nothin' else. (*Sits*)

REUBEN: You can talk, Emmett—but just stop that "killin'" business—we just saw Jinny stretched out on a table dead!

EMMETT: All right—(*Slight pause*) I guess y'all the bereaved family, huh? Well, I want you to know, I'm family too!

REUBEN: Nobody said nothin' about you not bein' in the family!

EMMETT: Y'all are not the only people gonna miss her—I was her godfather too, remember that! I carried her first bassinet down here on the train from New York. You have any idea what losin' Jinny did to us? There ain't that many of us left! Five— and Ash is Rachel's kin! (*He points to Victor*) That's the last Tate sittin' right there—and I'm not supposed to have something to say? I'll tell you what: If they come back through here again with they little gang war—I got something for 'em!

REUBEN: Come on, Emmett—that's enough, now.

EMMETT: What's wrong with you? I can remember the time I'd-a had to hold him back—nobody messed with the Tates! Thing like this happen, your father and the rest of us would be on the street until we caught the little sons-a-bitches, and took an eye for an eye!

REUBEN: We're not headhunters. This is not the old days! Emmett—you livin' in the past!

EMMETT: You changed when you got married.

REUBEN: Emmett, the next goddamn thing you say, I'm puttin' your ass back on the train to New York!

EMMETT: I just may go!

REUBEN: Then go, damnit!

RACHEL: Will y'all stop it please? Please? All this wild talk is not gonna bring Jinny back.

(*There is a moment of silence*)

REUBEN: Why don't you get us both a beer, Emmett? It'll cool us off. Is there still beer in the box, honey?

RACHEL: There's some in there.

REUBEN: Get me a cold one, OK?

(*Emmett rises*)

EMMETT: I still think I got a right to say something. (*Softer*) I'm sorry, Rachel. And I didn't mean that about you, Victor.

(*Victor nods as Emmett starts out. There is a slight pause*)

VICTOR: What was Uncle Emmett talkin' about, Dad?

REUBEN: Aw, mess happened before you was born. I was boxing then. Stuff not worth repeatin'. (*To Rachel*) You all right?

RACHEL: (*Nods*) Got a slight headache, though.

REUBEN: Did you take any aspirins?

RACHEL: (*Nods*) But too many of them, and they work on my stomach. (*Reuben reaches for her*) I'm all right . . . but it just happened . . . and it's hard to get over, Reuben!

REUBEN: (*Gently*) Rachel, come on now—

VICTOR: Can I go out?

(*Rachel is suddenly terrified*)

RACHEL: No!

REUBEN: Relax!

RACHEL: Where's he gonna go? Out on the same street, so they can kill him too? (*To Victor*) No! You stay in here—we just got back into the house. You just stay in.

VICTOR: I wanna go out, Mom!

RACHEL: I said, no!

VICTOR: Just on the front steps—I want to be by myself!

RACHEL: We need to be together at a time like this—your father's here—

REUBEN: (*Firmly, overlapping*) Go out, son.

(*Victor rises quickly*)

RACHEL: I don't want him out there, Reuben.

REUBEN: He's got a right to his own way of handling this thing, Rachel! (*To Victor*) You heard me, son; go 'head. (*Victor starts out*) Everybody's got their own way—let him grieve any way he wants to.

RACHEL: Let him grieve in this house and live! Victor!

VICTOR: (*Stopping*) What?

REUBEN: Damnit, leave him alone, Rachel!

RACHEL: (*After pause*) Well, he better not get off those steps then—(*Loud*) You stay around those steps out there, Victor! You hear me? In fact, don't go off the steps!

REUBEN: (*Shaking his head*) Stay around the steps, son.

VICTOR: All right.

RACHEL: That's right—around those steps. (*She is quiet for a moment*) This morning, she got up—took her forever to get her clothes on. She messed around with her food—started an argument with Victor—broke the last of those glasses I got from Ash. I told her I was going to call you if she kept it up. But I made her go outside, Reuben—I made her!

REUBEN: This is not your fault.

RACHEL: She just got on my nerves so bad—She wouldn't listen! I

9

told her three times to clean up that mess she left in her room —three times! (*Quietly*) You shoulda been here.

REUBEN: I'm here now—and I was here the weekend—

RACHEL: (*Interrupting*) Are you going to stay this time—or leave —or what? Because I really can't take it, Reuben! It's too much to ask me to do by myself right now—I can't deal with this and not know what's on your mind!

(*Emmett re-enters with the beer in glasses, Reuben and Rachel stop abruptly*)

EMMETT: (*Noticing*) I brought you some beer, Rachel—it's cool, in this heat it'll make you feel better—Vic didn't leave on account of me, did he?

REUBEN: No.

EMMETT: Good! It's got to be tough on him too! (*Hands the beers out*) You know they startin' to sell Budweiser on the trains now? (*Reuben and Rachel sip*) They're nice and cold, Reub!

RACHEL: Thank you, Emmett—I'm just—(*Leans back saddened again*) I just feel so damn empty! I keep expecting her to come stomping down the stairs—or hear her disco music playing through that upstairs hall! How do you get used to an empty room? (*Pause*) Reuben? You remember the time she put on all my makeup? You shoulda seen her that day, Emmett—lipstick from one end of her face to the other—rouge everywhere— powder in her hair—cologne all over her dress—(*Shakes her head*) She was so much a girl!

REUBEN: Don't make yourself upset, baby—

RACHEL: I want to remember! She was born February tenth, weighed eight and a half pounds, and had a star-shaped birthmark on the heel of her right foot—(*To herself*) I don't know why she had that—I don't have one—and she didn't cry right away when they slapped her—did you know that, Emmett? (*Emmett seems embarrassed*) When Reuben first saw her, he said she looked like my side of the family, didn't you, Reuben? And she was easier than Victor. It was almost like she couldn't wait to pull herself out of me.

REUBEN: Rachel.

RACHEL: I'm all right. I was just telling Emmett what I remember, he don't mind.

REUBEN: I think you should lay down.

RACHEL: I can't rest! How can I rest? Or just take aspirins? I keep seeing her crossing the room, Reuben—sitting in that chair—or that one! Or coming through the door.

(*Reuben gestures to Emmett*)

REUBEN: Baby, you hafta lay down—Emmett, help me. (*Reuben rises*)

RACHEL: She's the baby, Reuben—how could they take the baby? (*She begins to cry again as Reuben reaches for her*)

REUBEN: Rachel, come on now—I want you to lay down. Don't argue, you need the rest. You'll feel better.

RACHEL: (*Nods*) Yes, I need the rest. (*Reuben and Emmett guide her up and start her toward the stairs, as Russell, a friend of Victor's, enters from stage right, sees Victor and slowly starts in his direction*) You call Ash.

REUBEN: Called her when we first got in. She's on her way.

RACHEL: She loves Jinny so much. I'm glad you're home, Reuben.

REUBEN: Shhh! You just hold on to me.

(*They move up slowly. Emmett goes part way, then returns to living room alone*)

RUSSELL: (*Stopping at the steps*) Hey, blood!

VICTOR: Hey, Russ.

RUSSELL: I'm sorry about your sista man. (*Slight pause*) Word is, it was two dudes from the Bottom.

VICTOR: Who?

RUSSELL: (*Shrugs*) But a dude named Zooman runs it downtown. They say he's a little crazy. Tommy tol' me, Zooman and his brother Kenny beat up they own Mom—said they caught her comin' out the bar, and dusted her. That's his own mother!

(*Victor is silent*)

VICTOR: (*Finally says to Russell*) Can you get me a gun?

RUSSELL: (*Surprised*) You want a burner? (*Victor nods*) I guess I know how you feel, Vic—but Ward got the bullets.

VICTOR: Can you get the gun now?

RUSSELL: (*Nods*) It'll take awhile though. I hide it in my Mom's room, (*Reuben and Emmett emerge from the room*) and she's been in bed sick since they shot—you know, since the shooting. It really shook her up, man. Everybody around here liked Jinny. You goin' in? (*Victor nods*) I'll see you later—I'll git it though.

(*Russell starts away. A quiet settles over things as Victor eventually re-enters and sits quietly. Awkwardly Reuben and Emmett try to talk*)

REUBEN: How was the trip from New York?

EMMETT: Same. How's the bus company?

REUBEN: (*Shakes his head*) They call theyself upgradin' the systems . . . got all new buses. The old ones had that handle—you reached over, threw the handle forward and the front doors opened. When the last person got off the bus in the back, the back doors swung back into position, shut and locked. But these new buses—you got one button to operate the whole system. And the damn thing never works—I have to get out of my seat, walk to the back of the bus and slam the right side of the back door before the damn thing will close! And they call that progress!

EMMETT: Ain't no different at Bellevue—they hire all these no-readin' niggahs, instead of teachin' 'em somethin'—the otha day, this kid been in my section 'bout four—five weeks, takes a bottle of acid off the shelf—how it got there I'll never know—pours it into a bucket, and damn if he don't start moppin' the floor with it! The damn tiles start turnin' brown—couple nurses shoes start burnin'. I caught it, but you know he told me he couldn't read—imagine that? Couldn't tell the difference between cleanin' compound and acid cause the two bottles look alike.

REUBEN: When do you have to go back to New York?

EMMETT: They told me I might have to be back Wednesday—it's vacation time, and I'm on call—plus most of those Brothers I'm workin' with don't know nothin' 'bout cleanin' hospital floors! Average one of 'em ain't neva even picked up a mop! (*Pause*) What about you?

REUBEN: The Union gets us a week for something like this—it's in the contract.

(*Emmett nods, and Reuben is quiet*)

EMMETT: (*Cutting across everything loudly*) I wanna do something, Reuben! Goddamnit!

REUBEN: (*Shoots back*) What? What, Emmett? Kill somebody? Damnit, let it be! (*Tries to calm him*) There's nothin' to do! Leave it to the police—them boys ran through here in broad daylight!

EMMETT: When you ever know the police to catch anybody, when you the victim?

(*Victor rises*)

VICTOR: I'm-a go upstairs, Dad.

REUBEN: All right, go ahead, son—look in on your mother, OK?

(*Victor nods and starts upstairs*)

VICTOR: Are you gonna stay, Dad?

REUBEN: I'll be here.

(*Victor continues up. There is a brief silence*)

EMMETT: When did you and Rachel start havin' problems?

REUBEN: Four—five months now.

EMMETT: All the times I called you niggahs on the phone, and you ain't neva said nothin' about it?

REUBEN: Emmett, goddamnit, it's none of your business!

EMMETT: It is my business! I'm in this family—it is my business!

(*Across the stage Donald Jackson walks toward the Tates' front door*)

REUBEN: This is not the time to talk about it!

14

RACHEL: *I keep seeing her, Reuben — feeling her all over the room. And I want to say something to her — reach out and straighten her hair, touch her dress. And I know she's gone —*

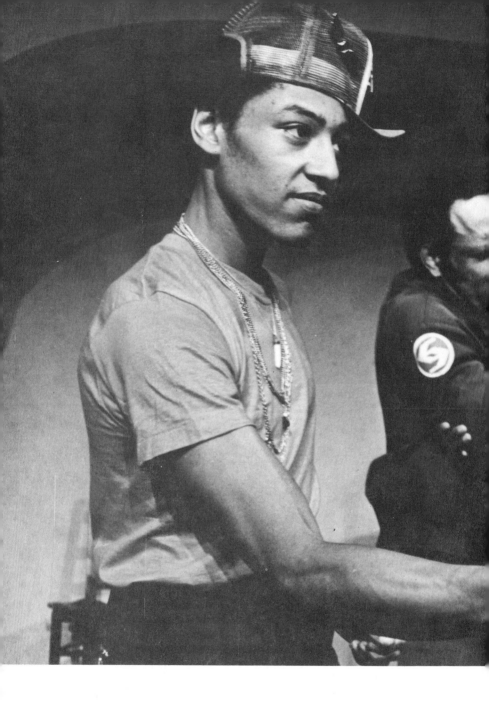

*EMMETT: I say we go out there — me and you, Reub, with two pistols, hunt the little bastards down and put a goddam bullet in each one of 'ems head!*

RUSSELL: *Don't play no martyr, Vic — you gettin' like your fatha'!*
*My Mom said, half these niggahs 'round here can't even read that*
*sign, and those that can, it just pisses them off, 'cause it brings the*
*whole neighborhood down....*

REUBEN: *Jackson — your wife? She saw the whole thing, didn't she?*

EMMETT: Y'all don't need no advice? You know everything?

(*The doorbell rings almost as a reprise. No one moves at first. Reuben and Emmett share looks at one another. The strain is beginning to take its toll of Reuben. The doorbell rings again. Reuben holds back his own tears*)

REUBEN: (*Gently*) Let me be, Emmett.

(*Emmett nods, he is ashamed of himself. He rises and starts to the door*)

EMMETT: I'll get it. (*Emmett goes to the door as Reuben sits quietly in his own grief. Emmett glances back at Reuben before opening the door*) Yes?

JACKSON: Hello, I'm Donald Jackson—I live down the street? I just came by to see if there was anything I could do?

EMMETT: (*Awkwardly*) Come in—Reub, Mr. Jackson's here—I'm Emmett Tate, Reuben's uncle.

(*The two men shake*)

REUBEN: (*Recovering, overlapping*) Hey, Jackson. (*Rises*) Come on in. (*Jackson takes a few steps past the door*) 'Xcuse the place.

JACKSON: It's all right, Reub. I been knowin' y'all since you moved 'round here—you don't have to be fancy with me! (*To Emmett*) I useta be a fan of his, when he boxed light-heavy—and—I took his missus to the hospital, when the little girl was born. Didn' I Reub? (*Reuben nods*) My wife, she come and got me that day—it was cold, I remember that—Reub was workin'—(*There is a slight pause*) They got me workin' split-shift this week—I go on nights next Thursday—and I tol' my wife I'd just come over for a hot minute, Reub, to see if there was anything I could do.

REUBEN: I appreciate it, Jackson.

JACKSON: My wife, she was in the back hangin' clothes when it happened. By the time she got to the front door, them boys was halfway up the block. She didn't see nothin'—and me, I was at work, Reub—but my wife said there was something y'all might want to know—

REUBEN: (*Quickly*) What?

JACKSON: Well—see by us livin' down at the end of the block, they got to us last—(*To Emmett*) See my house is actually on Master Street, but we never used that door—we always come out on the Titan Street side—it makes my house seem like the first house at that end of the street. Anyway, he didn't tell me, he told my wife, and she tol' me to tell Reuben. Cop told her he went to every house on the block and not one person claim they saw anything.

REUBEN: What!

JACKSON: That's what the cop said.

REUBEN: There's forty—fifty families around here!

JACKSON: It seemed strange to my wife too, 'cause she said when she came outside, everybody in the block was on their porch. About half on your side, and most of them on my side.

REUBEN: You sure that's what the cop said? (*Jackson nods*) And they covered every house?

EMMETT: They ain't shit, Reub!

REUBEN: That's impossible. Mrs. Smith sits on her porch morning till night. Davis stays at his window—he can't even get upstairs. I don't believe it!

16

RACHEL: (*Appearing on the stairs unnoticed*) Believe what?

REUBEN: (*Answering reflexively*) Nobody on the block says they saw anything.

RACHEL: What! They can't—they're lying!

REUBEN: (*Realizing it's her*) Rachel, you shouldn't be up—

RACHEL: I don't care what they say, they're lying! I saw them. They were all out there!

REUBEN: Maybe they too shocked to talk yet.

RACHEL: They'll tell me! I saw them. Mrs. Smith, Julius Williams—

REUBEN: Rachel—

RACHEL: I saw Mrs. Smith standing by her front door. I looked right at Julius Williams—and Davis, Mr. Cortez, ole man Washington!

REUBEN: Come on, baby—

RACHEL: Dottie Henson was hanging out her window! They're not blind! Let me talk to them—I'm her mother. They'll tell me! They'd better tell me! I swear before God they betta tell me!

REUBEN: Stop it, Rachel!

RACHEL: No! They wouldn't dare lie to me! (*Shouts*) I saw you, Dottie!

REUBEN: Rachel!

RACHEL: I saw the bitch, Reuben! How can she say she didn't see

it. They've got to tell me! They all saw it. They were all outside when those boys ran through here! They all watched her die!
(*Breaks down crying as Reuben attempts to restrain and comfort her*) Goddamnit, I saw them! I saw them! I saw them . . .

(*Reuben continues to hold Rachel as the lights go down in the
Tate residence and simultaneously Zooman's music begins to
rise. The light builds over the platform, where Zooman is standing. He is playing with his knife and almost listening to the
music; when it begins to fade, he is almost pleasant*)

ZOOMAN: When you got nothin' to do, come to the Zoo!
(*Quieter*) First couple hours are the worse. The big, blue fools
are probably sweeping the neighborhood by now, picking up everybody in sight. So there ain't that many mothafuckin places
to hide—except maybe in a junkie-hole—or out here in the
mothafuckin park—(*Pause*) I got someplace to go. I just don't
wanna' git nobody in trouble, that's all! You stay away from
your people as long as you can—besides, my Mom neva could
take pressure, no way! She'd just sit there and cry—plus, it's the
first damn place the mothafuckin Man is gonna look! I ain't
that dumb! (*Sudden mood swing*) I shot the little bitch 'cause
I felt like it! Zoo-man felt like shooting somebody! And that
mothafuckin Gustav is just lucky it ain't him! I got up this
mornin' and felt like killing somebody! So what? (*Beat*) I got
picked up twenty-one times las' year! Every time somebody
black did somethin' and the cops didn't have a name? They
busted me! Fuck y'all! Y'all don't lock up them dirty derelicts
on the street—shit-smellin' mothafuckas' hair all caked
with grease and slime—sleepin' in cardboard boxes, siftin'
through trash, talkin' to theyself—Beggin'! I try to set one of
them filthy mothafuckas on fire, every chance I get! (*Pause*)
Jive cunt call herself a teacher and come to school with her tit-
ties showin' every day, in an all-boys school—then gonna talk
shit, when they raped her. I was in Juvenile "D" eighteen
months, and I wasn' even in it! Here's a bitch been in the
school three years, and ain't neva looked at nobody! All young
niggahs look alike! So me and Stockholm do time because a

schoolteacher can't pick out the right boys—from her own fuckin' class, in a lineup! And Stockholm's a niggah with straight hair! Bitch neva taught us nothin'—but she's still there! They shoulda killed the bitch—then they'd-a caught the right people. (*Pause*) Tomorrow's *my* little sista's birthday! Not my sista here—a half sista in Birmingham—she'll be ten. She's down there with my fatha's people. I gotta 'notha half sista who's married. I got people everywhere. Detroit, California. I got an uncle in Buffalo—couple cousins in Houston. I got a aunt on my motha's side graduated top of her class at college —Plus I got friends in town! PJ, Mooky, Christine—so I got plenty of places to go if I want to! Plenty. (*Pause*) I just don't want to.

(*The light fades around Zooman, simultaneously with the lights building on the Tate household. It is after midnight and, though dark, the house seems less troubled than before, due mostly to a smallish woman [thin] in her late fifties. Her name is Ash Boswell and like Rachel she is dressed in a robe. But there the similarity stops. Ash is stylish and for her age a good-looking woman, her hair is done, her makeup in place despite the hour.*

*The phone is ringing and Ash picks it up as scene begins*)

ASH: Hello? Yes—no, this is her cousin—unhuh—it was a shock for everybody—unhuh. I'll tell them. Thanks for calling. (*Hangs up*) Somebody named Mason—lives down the street.

REUBEN: I'm tellin' you, Rachel, it was like they didn't know me! Mr. Davis, and Gibson down the street? They didn't even answer the door! And I could hear Gibson draggin' that bad leg of his across the floor! His screen door was closed but his front door was wide open—the TV was on! I go down the street to Julius Williams' house, and he acts like he didn't know we *had* a daughter! Not one damn person on the block claims they saw anything! The woman Rachel saw leanin' out her winda, Dottie Henson—and that boy Russell's mother claim they didn't even hear the shots!

RACHEL: They're lying!

REUBEN: I know.

ASH: It's a shame how we Negroes have changed through the years, honey—from one extreme to the next, like Jekyll and Hyde! (*Pause*) How was that uncle of yours when you passed through the dining room?

REUBEN: He's sleeping.

RACHEL: He drank quite a bit while you were gone.

ASH: Got sassy too, didn't he? (*Winks at Rachel*) If he wasn't family—a couple of those times he got out of hand, ole Ash woulda popped him upside his head! He's younger than I am by seven months, you know, so I can straighten his butt out quick, honey! (*Slight pause*) But I knew he was taking it pretty bad when I walked in here—he needs his sleep. You Tates get evil when you drink, honey. That's something we don't have on the Boswell side. (*Laughs, but Reuben is distracted, Ash notices*) What's the matter, Reuben?

REUBEN: (*Rising*) It's these people. What happens if the police catch the boys they think did it, and nobody comes forward to identify them? They go free?

ASH: Black people don't like to deal with the police, Reuben.

REUBEN: I'm not the police! Me and Rachel been livin' here fifteen—sixteen years! Jinny was born on this block! And they all act like strangers—what's wrong with them? All I've done for these people—Simpson, Edwards! Loaned Davis my tools— took him to the hospital—and I know he saw it! He sits in front of that goddamn window of his all day! The man's a cripple!—and in the summertime around here, you can't *get* these Negroes off they porches!

ASH: I blame a lot of this on them food stamps, honey.

REUBEN: Food stamps?

ASH: That's right! When the "Negro" was hungrier, we treated each other better. Nowadays everybody's got their bellies full and we sit up belchin', watching those damn soap operas and game shows all day—hot dog in one hand, the phone in the other, a beer—or a Pepsi—on the floor beside us, the baby crawlin' around dirty, the whole house filthy, and honey don't give a damn about nobody! You hear me? (*Slight pause*) When we knew we might have to borrow a cup of flour—or a pair of pants—or a white shirt from the people across the street, we were a lot more concerned about them, and a lot more conscientious about ourselves.

REUBEN: Now Ash—

ASH: What else is it then? There was a time when you didn't see black girls in their teens and early twenties fat and out of shape, honey! No indeed! These food stamps got all these children eatin' cookies, candy and potato chips! A woman reached her forties and fifties you'd understand the weight, but when I was young, honey, we took care of our figures—humph! Our bustlines and hips were legendary.

RACHEL: (*Gently*) But Ash, Reuben's—talkin' about somethin' else.

ASH: It's all the same—if they don't care about themselves, their own health, how they gonna care about you? Or Jinny or any of it?

REUBEN: It's not food stamps, all right? Not one food stamp answered anybody's door on this block, Ash!

(*Ash rises, a little hurt*)

ASH: I'll finish the dishes.

RACHEL: Just leave them, Ash. (*To Reuben*) You didn't have to holler.

REUBEN: I'm sorry, Ash.

ASH: It's all right. I know what kind of time this is—besides, I need to do something with my hands—take my mind off things. (*Saddens*) It's still hard for me to accept it. When your call came, I just sat in a chair beside the window thinking about her. Remember that time she came up to Boston? She went off in those people's hearts like a firecracker. My pastor, Reverend Daniels? He loved her—still talks about what a beautiful child she was. (*Suddenly distracted*) That reminds me, I'd better call him and ask him to send somebody over to my house. When I got up, I just ran out and jumped in the car—I'm not even sure I closed all the windows. (*Starts away*) But it's a shame is what it is—(*She exits and the room is quiet for a moment*)

RACHEL: Did you have any trouble getting away this afternoon?

REUBEN: (*Shakes head "no"*) I told Sid, the foreman, what happened and he let me go right away. How come you didn't go to work?

RACHEL: Inventory. They're bringing in the fall line—changing displays. Sometimes that department store is like a Zoo. (*Long pause*) Are you still seeing Florence?

REUBEN: I was never *seeing* Florence—I was with the woman one time!

RACHEL: I don't want to know about it!

REUBEN: You saw me with her—I told you I was sorry about that six months ago! I'm livin' in one room, Rachel, with one bed, one pillow—

RACHEL: I don't want my husband to be with other women!

REUBEN: I'm not going to say it no more—I'm not with no otha woman.

RACHEL: (*To herself*) You better not be! (*Slight pause*) I don't want my husband to do that—and I'm not saying you're not a good person—or good father. You do for us—the children love you and I love you, but I'll be damned if I let you live here with me and run around with other women! You are not going to do that to me!

REUBEN: I can't keep apologizing for it!

RACHEL: And I can't take it—not that and this too! I can't!

REUBEN: Then let it be! I feel bad enough, Rachel. I wasn't even here when it happened—I feel bad enough.

(*The room is quiet, Rachel softens*)

RACHEL: Jinny asked me yesterday if she could call you.

REUBEN: She called—she said you told her it was all right. I was glad you did that.

RACHEL: How did she sound?

REUBEN: Like Jinny, her mouth going non-stop, told me all about this new record she bought by the Commodores—and some book you said she could read, that was sexy, but not sexy enough for me to worry about—was she that old?

RACHEL: She had her first period a couple of weeks ago—you know what she said? Said she didn't like the blood—it got all

23

over everything, and did I think it would ever happen without all the blood. (*Pause*) She was laying in it, Reuben—it was all over the steps—and I wanted to save it—bring her back to life!

REUBEN: Try not to think about it!

(*He grabs her and holds her for a moment as she fights back tears, and nods taking several breaths. She is quiet for a moment*)

RACHEL: She said she wanted us back together again.

REUBEN: She said it to me too—I'm not going anywhere.

RACHEL: Reuben, why don't we move? We could spend more time together—I took the kids out to that shopping center out on Route 452? It's nice out there! And we're both working—this place is almost paid for, and in a few years if we stay, we won't be able to get our money back!

REUBEN: You know we can't move—the porch isn't paid for—we got a two hundred twenty-five-dollar car note—and it's week to week around here!

RACHEL: I don't want to live here anymore! You can't walk the streets—I'm sick of it! And nobody gives a damn! I even had to call the police myself—leave my baby and go to the phone, because I didn't hear a siren! They stood on their porches with their mouths open! What if it had been Grace's little girl, Denise? Or Mr. Davis' granddaughter Phyllis? Reuben, I want to move!

REUBEN: We can't go anywhere, until somebody around here says they saw something.

RACHEL: What are you gonna do, drag them outta their houses?

REUBEN: Emmett wasn't all wrong, in the old days I'd-a got them to say something or kicked their damned doors in!

RACHEL: And what would that prove?

REUBEN: I'm her father! I can't just sit here and do nothing!

RACHEL: Reuben you promised me—you're not a fighter anymore, you're a bus driver—

(*Ash enters*)

ASH: You all call me?

REUBEN: (*Quieter*) No Ash—(*He stares at Rachel, a little frustrated*)

ASH: I'm making potato salad, Rachel.

RACHEL: Ash, I don't want all that food! All the family we have is here, and I don't want these people in this neighborhood in my house, slopping down my food and staggering home drunk! We don't need any potato salad!

ASH: You don't need what?

RACHEL: You think I want them in my living room, sitting on my furniture—

ASH: I never heard of a black family in mourning in my life that didn't have potato salad for people who come by to pay their respects. Never in my life! It's bad manners! What are people supposed to eat?

REUBEN: Make the potato salad, Ash.

ASH: (*Nods*) Where's the relish?

REUBEN: I think it's in the refrigerator—in those shelves on the door.

(*Ash starts out, shaking her head*)

ASH: (*To herself*) I never heard of that in my life!

(*There is a long pause. Reuben and Rachel stare at one another for a while, but Rachel breaks their silence with a sudden painful outburst*)

RACHEL: (*On the verge of tears*) Reuben, I think I'm just gonna explode and die in a minute! And keep exploding—and dying, and dying—over, and over, and over—(*Reuben tries to comfort her*) My stomach's sour, Reuben! Where she was in my stomach is empty! And I'm sick! God, I'm so sick! I'm so sick!

(*The light begins to fade around the Tate household, rising slowly over the platform along with Zooman's music. Zooman steps slowly onto the platform, smiling*)

ZOOMAN: You know, I damn near got caught? Yeah. I go snatch this ole bitch's pocketbook, and she started yellin'—wig came off, and shit! I had to knock her down! Then this hero mothafucka chases my ass five blocks before I could duck into an all-night movie. (*Shakes head*) And sure enough, the big blues comes walking down the aisle shinin' a flashlight in everybody's face—and all these nasty mothafuckas with their flies open started jumpin' up coverin' their faces, cause the big blues came in while this bitch on the screen is screwin' four dudes, and half the scum in the movie have their funky-ass dicks out! (*Disgusted*) Sick mothafuckas! I acted like I had dropped somethin' but the man stood *right* there, till I straightened up —but just then this crazy Brother down front leaps up, starts shoutin' at the screen—"The day of judgment is coming! The day of judgment is coming!" Ran all up on the stage, waving a gun—callin' everybody filth—and the big blues took off afta him. Yeah. (*To himself*) I'm glad I got rid of that gun. "Magic" is all I need anyway. You shoulda seen that bitch when I stuck it in her face—she was lucky her pocketbook was all I took. You ain't expect me to eat out no garbage can, did you? (*Chuckles*) Bitch screamed her fuckin' head off! Help! Thief! (*Pause*) But they ain't caught Zooman yet. And they may never catch me.

## Act One

(*Light fades slowly around Zooman along with his music, and comes up on Reuben who is standing in "limbo" on the stage. He is dressed in his uniform and cap and is carrying a sign rolled up and tied. It is cloth*)

REUBEN: Some promises are hard to keep. Losing Jinny was like waking up and discovering the sun had a hole in it. She had the softest black skin I'd ever seen. Came out of her mother like an explosion, and had a way of smiling at you, made you feel somebody had given you a gift. She was an extension of me! I wanted to see her grown—bring a boy around here for me to meet—do something—be something! Twelve years old ain't nothin'! It took me fifteen years to get seniority on my job—twenty—thirty—years to grow up! Twelve years ain't nothin'! (*Confused*) I promised her life! We all did—or at least a chance! And right here! Not out on Route 452! Here, where her memory is. (*Slight pause*) But I made Rachel a promise too. I couldn't break it—and God knows I wanna beat somebody up! (*Slight pause*) So instead, I went downtown this morning, and had this sign made to hang over our porch. Get these folks off their asses. It sure can't hurt nobody. Not the way I could. But maybe it'll make somebody come forward.

(*Reuben starts away. The instant he exits, the light begins to fade around the house and the sign begins its descent over the stage. Painted on it are the words: THE KILLERS OF OUR DAUGHTER JINNY ARE FREE ON THE STREETS BECAUSE OUR NEIGHBORS WILL NOT IDENTIFY THEM! Light bathes the sign for one bright moment, then slowly begins to close around it, as the stage goes to black and a hint of Zooman's music begins to linger in the air*)

END OF ACT I

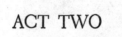

ACT TWO

# ACT II

## SCENE:

*As before. A window in the Tate home is broken and has been covered over with a piece of cardboard. There is a wreath on the front door, but the light builds around the platform, where now Rachel is standing. She looks tired, drawn, but she has changed into another blouse, skirt and shoes. She is now carrying a bag of groceries. She looks at the sign for a moment, then faces the audience.*

RACHEL: What is it about men, that won't let them leave well-enough alone? No one buried in a graveyard can read the inscription on their headstone! And this neighborhood is dead! (*She is quiet, remembering*) Reuben had quit prize fighting a year, before they hired him at the bus company. I was three months pregnant with Victor, and we went to Emmett and borrowed seven hundred dollars to make settlement on that house. Place only cost us seven-five, but in those days that was a lot of money! (*Smiles*) We didn't have a stick of furniture—Reuben never made no money in the ring. Reuben's mother—God rest her soul—gave us all she could, in a card table and two of those fold-up chairs. We ate off that until we bought

31

our first kitchen set—and had to use an old single bed for a couch. (*Slight pause*) This neighborhood was already black then and we never turned on ourselves—we kept the block clean, swept the sidewalks, gave our little block parties and watched out for each otha's kids. I could run to the store and leave my front door open. (*Pause*) The only stranger would be somebody who didn't live around here. (*Pause*) But I can remember the day, and the hour, that fool down at the end of the street, Julius Williams, began fixing used cars in the middle of the damn sidewalk, and the oil stains and dirt tracked their way through the entire block. And outside of Reuben and Mr. Neal up at the corner, nobody around here said or did anything! Couple months later they shot Scherr in the grocery store —the Armstead family across the street staged a gun-battle with the cops, then the riots closed all the stores on the Avenue, and gave the nighttime to the thieves! It's been like livin' on a burning fuse! (*Quietly*) Reuben can hang up all the signs he wants to—you can't bring the dead back to life. Not them— not Jinny. I just want to move.

(*Rachel starts toward the house, where the light is rising. Victor and Russell are in the living room. They are listening to music and watching a portable TV with the sound turned off*)

RUSSELL: I wouldn't do it, Vic. You got your whole life ahead of you, cutty! How you gonna make it to the pros if the cops lock you in the slams? Hello, Mrs. Tate.

RACHEL: Hello, Russell—Victor, turn that music down, please!

(*She passes through the room and exits on the right, as Victor turns the music down, grumbling*)

VICTOR: I can't even hear it!

(*Once he feels she is out of earshot, he turns the music up a trifle, and sits back down*)

RUSSELL: Homicide is a deep offense, Vic. And you know if you go to jail, they hafta send you to Trayburg, and I heard they like to make girls outta young guys like us. (*Victor waves disdainfully*) What could you do, if two-three old heads—say, dudes in their twenties and thirties jumped your ass and take it?

VICTOR: I'd kill somebody—or kill myself.

RUSSELL: Let the cops catch Zoo and those guys, man! Besides, you don't know that it's Zoo anyway—the rumor is that it was just some *guys* from the Bottom.

VICTOR: If he's the runner, I want him to know I'm after him too —maybe he'll give up the dudes that did it.

RUSSELL: (*Amused*) Paint a sign like your old man did! Hang it at the bottom of that one. (*Across the air in front of him*) "Zooman! I'm comin' to get you and your boys!" (*Laughs*) I'm sorry, Vic, but I never heard of anybody hanging up a sign like that before—the whole neighborhod is laughing—I saw a guy walk by it and fall out on the street, he was laughin' so hard! (*Teasing*) Did all those fights shake your ole man's thing loose?

VICTOR: It ain't funny, man—my father has his way—I have mine!

RUSSELL: What if Zoo and them kill you?

VICTOR: They'll just have to kill me then, OK?

RUSSELL: (*Annoyed*) Don't play no martyr, Vic—you gettin' like your fatha! My Mom said, half these niggahs 'round here can't even read that sign, and those that can, it just pisses them off, 'cause it brings the whole neighborhood down—'n somebody's always claimin' our people ain't no good. And even if you saw what happened, don't nobody like to deal with the cops. So she don't see why your father put it up in the first place, unless he's just trying to call attention to himself, like you tryin' to do.

VICTOR: You better stop making fun of my father, Russell—unless you want to fight. (*He rises and turns the TV off*)

RUSSELL: I didn't say nothin' 'bout your ole man—I tol' you what my Mom said. Mr. Williams said it too! (*Pause*) Hey, I'm tryin' to save your life, cutty! Because, I'm not gonna help you kill nobody—Zooman or anybody else!

VICTOR: (*Surprised*) You're not getting the bullets from Ward?

RUSSELL: Nope! They sell bullets in the hardware store, my man —Sears! In fact, I'm sorry I gave you the gun!

VICTOR: You're not getting it back.

RUSSELL: It's not worth a fight, Vic—just leave me out of it.

VICTOR: You're out of it.

RACHEL (*Offstage*): (*At once*) Victor?

VICTOR: Huh?

RACHEL: Is your father upstairs?

(*Ash emerges at the head of the stairs*)

ASH: (*Overlapping to Victor*) Is that your mother?

(*A woman Rachel's age, Grace Georges, in curlers, dungarees and T-shirt, strolls toward the front door. She will look at the sign, read it for a moment, then shake her head before crossing the porch to the door*)

VICTOR: (*To Ash*) She's looking for my father. (*Loud*) He went

34

to Buster's Bar—him and Uncle Emmett! Said he'd be right back.

RACHEL: (*Still offstage*) Where'd this potato salad come from?

ASH: (*Starting down*) That man Jackson—said his wife made some more—just in case. It's the second batch he's brought over here. He came while you were at the store. He acts funny to me! (*Grace rings the doorbell, Ash looks toward the door*) Who is this?

RACHEL: (*Offstage*) You're too suspicious, Ash.

ASH: (*Moving toward door*) I think that Jackson knows something about the shooting.

(*Doorbell rings again*)

GRACE: (*Outside at once*) Rachel. It's me honey, Grace!

RACHEL: (*As Ash opens door*) Let her in!

ASH: (*Simultaneously*) Hello!

RUSSELL: (*Rises*) I gotta go, cutty—my Mom wants to know when the wake is.

(*Grace steps inside smiling at Ash*)

GRACE: (*Overlapping*) I'm Grace Georges, a friend of Rachel's from down the street?

VICTOR: Tuesday—Lincoln Funeral Home.

(*Grace moves into the living room area*)

RUSSELL: (*Starting out*) You're wrong, Vic.

VICTOR: She wasn' your sista.

GRACE: Hi, Russell.

RUSSELL: Hello, Mrs. Georges. (*Russell and Victor move toward the door*) See you later, Vic.

(*Ash has followed Grace into the living room, where Grace is standing*)

ASH: Have a seat, hon, she'll be out in a minute—I'm her cousin, Ash Boswell.

GRACE: Pleased to meet you. Hi, Victor.

VICTOR: (*Closes door and starts to dining room*) Hello.

GRACE: I'm sorry about your sister.

(*Rachel emerges as Victor smiles faintly at Grace, passing his mother on his way offstage. Rachel seems a little tired*)

VICTOR: I'm-a get something to eat.

RACHEL: (*Nods*) Hi, Grace.

GRACE: How you feelin', girl? I just dropped by to pay my respects. Denise started to come over, but she's feelin' a bit under the weather—asthma's botherin' her in this heat, chile. Mike said he'd see Reuben at the Layout—he's got to work.

(*Rachel goes to the record player and turns it off, before sitting down*)

ASH: (*To Grace*) Can I get you a little plate of something? We've got plenty of potato salad, and I'm fixin' some greens—and chicken—and cornbread.

GRACE: Nawww—nooope, I'd better not. Mike'll be home soon and if I eat over here, I sure won't feel like standin' in front of no hot stove cooking his dinner—No, thank you. Girl, the way that man loves to eat, he'd have a shit fit! I'm not going to stay that long. (*Ash shrugs*) Girl, I guess you've just about run outta line, huh? (*Rachel nods*) It's a shame, Rachel. I think I woulda went out of my mind if it hada been Denise—I don't know how you can stand it. They'd-a had to carry me to the hospital—somethin'! My only child? They'd-a had to strap me down! (*Pause*) I am really sorry it happened, Rachel. If you need anything, just send Victor—or anybody!

RACHEL: Thanks, Grace—Ash came to help me out.

GRACE: (*To Ash*) My little girl, Denise, and Jinny useta play together. Rachel is strong—if it hada been Denise—and the way Mike loves that child? They mighta had to strap us both down! Men always love their little girls the most. (*There is an awkward moment of silence*) Well, I didn't intend to stay long.

(*Grace starts to rise*)

RACHEL: You don't have to rush, Grace.

(*Grace sits*)

GRACE: I didn't lock my front door, girl—but I did want to ask you one thing. (*Lower*) Why did you let Reuben hang that sign up, Rachel? He's got these people around here climbing the walls! Don't none of them appreciate it—in fact, Cortez and Williams told Mike they were planning to hold a block meeting about it. (*Pause*) And the truth is, I kinda think it makes the whole street look bad myself. You know what I mean? Like, what if you didn't see it? Thing like that lumps the good with the bad—and every time you turn around black folks are saying something terrible about each other! "We can't get together—our men ain't no good—we're triflin', everywhere we live is a slum!" I get tired of it myself—and Reuben's sign makes this look like the worse place in the world.

ASH: But then you didn't lose your little Denise, did you, honey?

GRACE: If we had, I wouldn't have let Mike advertise about it! That's y'alls private business!

RACHEL: Seems like a killing on the block would be everybody's business . . .

GRACE: The Tates ain't no better than nobody else! Rachel and Reuben didn't come to Myrtle Coleman's layout—or to Mr. Stewart's funeral either! I didn't see the Tates get excited when those hoodlums raped Lou Jefferson's little girl—or robbed my place! Why should anybody go out of their way for them? I didn't hang up no sign!

RACHEL: Did you see it, Grace?

GRACE: (*Stiffens defensively*) What? No! Don't you accuse me!

(*Two bricks crash against the screen door, break and splatter. A bottle breaks beside them. Grace screams at the crash. At once, Victor enters suddenly and crosses the room quickly to the front door*)

VICTOR: (*Incredulous*) They tryin' to knock the door down!

(*Victor moves to the door and simultaneously Rachel is up, frightened but unable to move. Ash follows him to the door*)

ASH: Stay in here, boy!

(*Victor is outside, where he pulls the gun. Ash sees him, Rachel cannot*)

GRACE: (*Interjecting*) I knew this would happen!

ASH: What are you doing with that, Victor? He's got a gun!

RACHEL: What gun? (*Moving*) Victor?

ASH: (*Overlapping*) Git in here! (*Opens the screen door*)

VICTOR: No.

RACHEL: (*Reaches door*) Give me that thing!

VICTOR: Suppose they come through here again? What do we do then? We need protection, Mom! The Tates just don't let people mess with them!

(*Rachel steps onto the porch and charges*)

RACHEL: You give me that damn gun right now! (*She snatches at it*) You give it to me! You hear me? (*She swings at him and snatches it*) Damn you, Victor! Are we supposed to lose you too?

(*Victor is immediately sorry, as Rachel looks at the gun with a mixture of horror and rage*)

ASH: (*Quickly*) Boy, get in here and get a broom and clean this mess up off the floor!

(*Victor starts past Rachel and she lashes out*)

RACHEL: (*Hitting him, in tears*) Don't you eva! (*Victor moves past her quickly*) I'll knock the living hell outta you! You hear me, Victor?

VICTOR: Yes.

(*Victor exits offstage, as Ash holds the door for Rachel as she enters. She hands the gun to Ash*)

RACHEL: Throw this thing in the trash!

ASH: Where in the name of hell did he get it?

GRACE: It's goin' to get worse, Rachel. People don't like being accused when they haven't done anything!

RACHEL: Get the hell out of here, Grace—Get out! (*Grace, angry, starts out without a word. She goes to the door, stops for a moment to look at Ash and Rachel, then exits. In the house, there is a moment of quiet*) Glass all over the porch! Did you hear him—The Tates! Will somebody please tell me what good that sign is accomplishing? Are we supposed to take turns sitting guard on the front steps? We're supposed to be in mourning for our daughter—there's a wreath on the door, and where the hell is he? Comes back three days, disrupts everything—turns things inside out. Putting up signs, it's—it's disrespectful! (*To herself*) I almost wish I had let him beat up a few of them.

ASH: No you don't.

RACHEL: I don't want this! (*Victor re-enters with a broom and dustpan*) I'm sick of you, Victor—give me that broom and go someplace outta my sight!

(*She snatches the broom and starts outside. Victor starts back in and heads upstairs*)

ASH: Are you all right?

RACHEL: (*Outside sweeping*) I'm fine! Just fine! (*Ash starts toward the dining room looking at the gun and shaking her head*) (*To herself*) I didn't go to Mr. Stewart's funeral because Reuben wasn't here! And he wasn't here when the Jefferson girl got raped—and I get tired of walking around by myself or with my kids, Reuben! Florence wasn't the first one! (*She bends over and picks up the debris*) What kinda people would do something like this?

(*She starts in, leaving the broom behind. From the right Reuben and Emmett emerge. It is clear they have been in a fight. They both seem in pain, Emmett holding his arm, Reuben's hand wrapped with a handkerchief. They both have trouble making it up to the porch. However, once Reuben sees the debris his own pain is unimportant. He reaches for the door and enters immediately leaving Emmett behind him*)

REUBEN: Rachel? What the hell happened?

(*Rachel re-enters, sees him and is shocked*)

RACHEL: Oh, my God!

(*Emmett enters*)

REUBEN: (*Quickly*) I'm all right. We got into a fight at Buster's
—what happened?

ASH: (*Re-entering*) Some fools threw a couple bricks at the door
—(*Rachel leads Reuben to the sofa*) Probably some nasty kids
—what happened to you two?

RACHEL: A fight at Buster's!

EMMETT: We turned that bar, OUT! (*He staggers in and flops
into a chair*) Didn' we, Reub?

(*Ash moves to him*)

RACHEL: Did you have to get into a fight?

REUBEN: What choice did I have?

EMMETT: (*Overlapping*) We didn' have no choice, Rachel!
(*Aside*) Pure case of survival.

ASH: (*Quickly*) You half drunk!

(*Emmett makes a face at her*)

REUBEN: We were drinking two beers—and this fella from Cro-
skey Street—I've seen him before. He walks up in *my* face, and
tells *me*, HE didn't want us in there—unless I took my sign
down! (*Mimics*) "You givin' the black community a bad
name!" Here's a man, in my face, for no reason, and I'm givin'
the community a bad name? (*Quieter*) I tol' him, I wasn't
takin' nothin' down, until it got some results!

41

EMMETT: Then the other guy punched me—and Reub punched him, and it was on!

(*Victor emerges*)

ASH: Hold still and let me look at this arm, fool!

REUBEN: (*Overlapping*) Help me get this jacket off, honey?

(*Rachel helps him reluctantly*)

VICTOR: What's goin' on?

EMMETT: Hey, nephew—me and your fatha was in a fight! You shoulda see him . . . He's still got a mean left hook!

RACHEL: You know how crazy you sound? Two grown men bragging?

REUBEN: Who's bragging? We didn't start it!

RACHEL: Is that where Victor got it—

REUBEN: What'd you expect me to do, Rachel?!

RACHEL: —pointing a gun all over the porch.

REUBEN: What?!—A gun!

RACHEL: A gun, that's what!

REUBEN: What were you doing with a gun, Victor—where'd you get it?!

RACHEL: Why weren't you here to find out?!

VICTOR: I found it.

REUBEN: Where?!

VICTOR: It wasn't loaded!

RACHEL: You had no business with it!

REUBEN: You want me to let loose on you boy?!

(*The phone interrupts as Ash also chimes in*)

ASH: This arm feels broken to me.

EMMETT: I been workin' in hospitals all my life! If it was broken, I'd know if it was broke!—

ASH: (*Exploiting the occasion to rescue Victor. To Emmett*) Come on you ole fool, let me see if I can do anything with this. You ain't got the sense you was born with. Like I said, you Tates is one evil bunch when you drink. (*To Victor*) Come on and help me, boy!

(*Victor rushes to obey. They exit as Reuben goes to answer the insistent phone*)

REUBEN: Hello? Yes this is Reuben Tate . . . Say that to my face, punk! Come around here and say that to my face! (*He slams the phone down*)

RACHEL: So now you're inviting them!

REUBEN: Rachel, I'm not going to stand around while people beat us the hell up! (*The phone interrupts again. This time, Reuben rushes to grab it*) Listen here, you—??? What? Channel 22? Yes, this is the Tate's residence. You're talking to him. Channel 22? Well, I hung it the other day. But I've never been on TV before, what would I say? Unhuh—just talk about the sign? Guess so—can't hurt. Unhuh. Well, I'd have to think about it—give me a day—I'll let you know. Sure, thanks for calling. (*He hangs up*) They heard about the sign and want to interview me.

RACHEL: I'm sick of that sign!

REUBEN: What's wrong with the sign?

RACHEL: We're supposed to be in mourning—We lost Jinny three days ago—why are you doing this now?

REUBEN: Rachel, that sign hasn't hurt anybody unless they feel guilty—it doesn't fire bullets—punch out people—

RACHEL: It is making people hate us, Reuben!

REUBEN: (*Angrily*) That's because there's not *enough* signs! I'm-a put up more of 'em—saturate the whole neighborhood! Telephone poles—store windows—buses—let everybody know! They want to be nasty?

RACHEL: You're making this a sideshow!

REUBEN: The sideshow was the day they ran through here, shot up the street, killed our daughter, and nobody on this block did anything about it! I'm not gonna let them forget Jinny's life!

RACHEL: Jinny? Who the hell is that? Guns, fights, signs on telephone poles—TV interviews and all in the name of Jinny? Hallelujah! Well *Jinny* was gentle, Reuben—did you forget that? A shy child—and this is her time! The last little bit of her time we have left, and someone in this family better pay her some attention, you know that? Somebody better pay some attention to her!

(*Reuben starts to reply, but is interrupted by the reappearance of Ash, Emmett and Victor. They enter urgently, Emmett obviously in deep pain, bent over holding his bruised arm, which has been wrapped in an improvised sling bandage*)

ASH: Come on, Reuben, we gotta drive him to the hospital. He's getting worse. I know his arm is broken.

(*Reuben rushes to Emmett's side. He and Victor help him toward the door, with Ash following behind. They exit as fast as they can, leaving Rachel alone in the house*)

RACHEL: (*Quietly to no one in particular*) Somebody needs to pay more attention to Jinny . . .

(*Lights fade out and rise upon Zooman once more at the platform*)

ZOOMAN: It's no fun being on the run. But I happen to know, if a black kills a black, and they don't catch you right away, they liable to forget about it—

One time, me an' Stockholm dodged the big blue fools for ten days.We holed up in a junkie-hole right 'round the corner from where we robbed the dude! Nighttime, we useta go out, ride the bus crosstown, break into a store or somethin', then get on the same bus and come back. Like Robin Hood! Sometime we just laid-dead and got high—Christine would sneak in with chicken and shit from Kentucky Fried. (*Pause*) I been goin' with Christine almost two years—she ain't got no kids of mine yet, but she says she wants one—

But Christine can't half take care of the kid Arnold gave her—little mothafucka be dirty all the time, smellin' like pee, and Christine be layin' up on the bed watchin' television—besides, she ain't got as much education as I got! (*Slight pause*) I ain't really worried yet. But that niggah with them signs? Ain't nobody ever pulled that kinda shit before! Killings, rapes, drugs —all kinds of shit be goin' on every day and nobody says nothin'! That section was always run-down and dangerous— Vacant junkie-holes everywhea, trash on the streets—(*Shakes head*) Always some mothafucka wanna be a hero! Wasn' neva no stores on the Avenue! You have to go half way around the world to get to the Chinese laundry—get your clothes cleaned, or your shoes fixed! Ain't nothin' in there but barbershops and junky corner groceries—and every now and then a drugstore where the man sells you your pills and cough syrup behind a bulletproof glass! Shiiiittt! The first junkie I ever met was a mothafucka lived 'cross the street—and I know every mothafucka that's stealin', muggin', hustlin' and procurin'—grew up with all of 'em! Everybody I know buys hot clothes! Curtis' mother? Walkin' around passin' out all that Let-Jesus-Save-You shit? Buys truckloads of hot dresses and be sellin' them to her Holy-Moly congregation. And I've seen Greenie's fatha stealin' cookies out the supermarket—puttin' tuna fish and shit under his coat!

Now he's gonna make that Zoo a neighborhood puttin' everybody on me?

The little bitch was in the way, that's all! Who the fuck he think he is? Sendin' people afta me, like I'm some animal! If he wants to blame somebody—you don't leave no little girl sittin' on her steps by herself nowadays! I don't let my sista go out by herself. He shoulda known better—what kinda fatha is he? (*Slight pause*) But I'll tell you what—if somebody don't git his ass straight soon, I'm-a show him just what a killer is— Niggahs can't be heroes, don't he know nothin'?

(*Zooman's music comes up for a moment, then begins to fade as the light around him goes to black. Simultaneously the light builds around the Tate household. Reuben, Emmett, Rachel and Victor cross the stage. Emmett's arm is in a sling and cast. They are all dressed in black. Ash, as they enter, emerges from the dining room area. Reuben leads Rachel to the sofa and sits beside her. It is evening*)

ASH: How was the service?

(*Victor and Emmett sit*)

REUBEN: Not much you can say about a wake, Ash. They said the prayers, blessed the casket—one little girl got up and read a little poem from her school, but there's not that much to say about a wake.

EMMETT: What was that preacher's name, Reub?

REUBEN: Walker—Reverend Walker.

EMMETT: (*To Ash*) He gave a good eulogy. It made me feel better—he didn' have the whole place cryin'!

(*Rachel sobs*)

VICTOR: (*At once*) You all right, Mom?

(*She nods*)

EMMETT: (*Continuing*) Like the way he talked about kids—and heaven, you didn't feel weighted down.

RACHEL: (*Overlapping*) I'm just numb, son.

(*Slight pause*)

EMMETT: At least it felt that way to me.

REUBEN: (*To Ash*) Your old girlfriend Mrs. Rheinhard was there. She asked about you.

ASH: Really? That was nice of her—how'd she look? The last time I talked to her, she was complainin' about her arthritis.

REUBEN: She looked all right to me.

EMMETT: (*Out of nowhere*) Children must be spared hell's fire, 'cause they're innocent. You hear that, Reub?

REUBEN: (*Nods*) A couple of the drivers I work with were there— and Lefty Cohen, my old trainer—did you see him? Rachel? Honey, you want an aspirin?

(*Rachel shakes her head "no"*)

47

ASH: Did they sing?

EMMETT: "Nearer My God To Thee"—all the standard stuff. (*To Reuben*) What was that one Jinny liked so much?

REUBEN: "Amazing Grace."

EMMETT: They sung that. It was a nice service, I thought. (*Looks around*) Jinny looked peaceful.

REUBEN: I was just thinking about her—she'd be sleeping by now —only child I ever saw slept with a smile on her face.

VICTOR: Didn't look nothin' like her to me. Why'd they put all that powder on her face?

REUBEN: That's just how they do it, son.

RACHEL: Other undertakers don't make people look like that, and you know it! I've been to enough wakes—(*Almost crying*) and the people didn't look like that!

REUBEN: What can we do about it now—take her someplace else?

RACHEL: That's not funny!

REUBEN: (*Gently*) I didn't like it any more than you did.

RACHEL: The whole thing was just so ugly!

(*Reuben puts his arm around her*)

ASH: Y'all got to forgive me for not going—I started to after you left, but I couldn't. I didn't want to see her like that. I sat here trying to find something to do—I even laid down to rest, and was surprised when the doorbell woke me up that I had fallen asleep. I dreamed about her. She was standing there, by the window, smiling. It startled me, it seemed so real.

48

EMMETT: We understand. (*To Reuben*) Who sent that big wreath? The one with twelve carnations on it?

REUBEN: I think her class took up a collection—I was surprised to see a bouquet from the block committee. Ash? Who came to the door—you said somebody woke you up?

ASH: That man who's been bringing all that potato salad over here—Jackson. This time he brought a pot of greens—said he wanted to talk to you and Rachel. He acts funny to me.

REUBEN: What did he do?

ASH: Nothin'—I don't know—he just acts funny—like he wants to say something and never says it! He's been back and forth over here every day—he acts like he's got things botherin' him. When I asked him to come in, he almost ran off the porch.

EMMETT: Maybe he saw something, Reub.

REUBEN: Jackson was at work.

EMMETT: Maybe his wife saw something—she's the one makin' all the food—and he keeps comin' by to see if anybody else came forward. You know we don't like to stick our necks out— and he acted strange to me, the first time he came by.

REUBEN: She does have a clear view of the street from her yard— maybe she did see it. She could be scared. They both might be.

EMMETT: They probably tryin' to get out of it!

ASH: He said he'd be by later.

REUBEN: (*To Emmett*) Everybody ain't like that! A whole lot of them came to the wake.

RACHEL: Well, which ones raised all the hell, Reuben?

REUBEN: Those people were ignorant—Smith, Williams and Judson wasn' never worth a damn!

EMMETT: (*Overlapping*) Anybody want a beer? Reub?

(*Reuben nods*)

RACHEL: (*As Emmett rises*) They whispered about his sign all through the whole damn service.

ASH: (*At once*) You don't need no more to drink, mistah.

(*Emmett waves at her disdainfully as he leaves*)

RACHEL: (*To Ash*) They wrote threats—and, and filth in the register! (*She holds up the book*) The only thing we got left! The layout register! You ever in your life hear of anything as rotten and lowdown as that? (*She throws it down*)

REUBEN: You know some kids wrote that—look at the handwriting! A lot of people came over to me and said they were glad about the sign—

RACHEL: Is Davis a kid? (*To Victor*) Tell your father what he told you—

VICTOR: He just said he was sorry about Jinny, and he thought the sign would bring us trouble.

REUBEN: I didn't hear him say that.

VICTOR: He was in the line—he leaned over and whispered it to me. (*Emmett re-enters, carrying beer*) Uncle Emmett heard it.

EMMETT: (*Handing out beers*) Yeah, I heard it. I tried to tap him with this cast a couple times, too!

RACHEL: Did you hear Julius Williams shouting all over the sidewalk?

REUBEN: Julius Williams ain't gonna do a damn thing—he is nothin' but mouth. If he even lights a cigarette in front of this house, I'll have him locked up!

RACHEL: And if someone else decides to set fire to it?

ASH: Fire?

RACHEL: They were threatening to burn the damn place down!

REUBEN: Then let 'em! I'm not taking down that sign because some drunken bum like Williams got loud!

(*Across the stage Jackson emerges. He is carrying several home-made loaves of bread. He moves toward the front door, stopping to look at the sign*)

EMMETT: Reub, I think I know how you feel, but people ain't like they used to be, they do vicious things nowadays, Reub. You got this to protect.

(*The doorbell rings. Ash starts up*)

REUBEN: That sign doesn't come down until someone comes forward.

(*Ash opens the door*)

ASH: Mr. Jackson!

(*Everyone turns around. Reuben rises and goes to the door, but Jackson doesn't come in. He remains by the door*)

REUBEN: Jackson, come on in!

JACKSON: No thanks, I'm on my way to work. I just came by to bring this bread my wife made. (*He hands it to Ash as Reuben approaches*) She said she knew y'all would be havin' company, and we both—me and my wife—figured Rachel would have enough to do.

51

REUBEN: Thanks.

JACKSON: I came by earlier—how's your missus?

REUBEN: OK. (*There is a slight awkward silence, Jackson is uneasy*) Jackson—your wife? She saw the whole thing, didn't she?

JACKSON: What? (*Surprised and hurt*) No, Reuben!

ASH: Ask him why he's been comin' over here so much then?

JACKSON: (*To Ash and Reuben*) My wife and me thought y'all needed a little help—I—My wife's been after me to tell y'all how we felt about you and the little girl. I came and took Rachel to the hospital when she was born. I—but I just couldn't say it. I tol' my wife, I said, "Sayin' something like that to people can embarrass a man!" But I figured if I brought something ova—a little gift or something—I wouldn' have to say it, 'cause y'all would know. But she kept pesterin' me—"You ain't said it!" She said that every day—and it was on me, 'cause I took her to the hospital.

REUBEN: Jackson, I—

JACKSON: Let me say it, all right? We like y'all! You and Rachel raised nice kids, and y'all ain't loud and don't raise a whole lotta hell around here! And I'm glad you put up that sign, but we didn't see nothin'—my wife or me. (*Indignant*) We ain't them kinda people, Reuben! (*Slight pause*) They come by my house this evenin' to ask me if me and my wife would join some march they plannin'. A group of 'em intend to pull that sign down, or set it on fire. I don't want no part of it! But we— (*Pause*) It's gettin' kinda late, and I gotta go to work. Tell your missus that bread's an easy recipe. My wife said, if she wants it, she'll give it to her. (*Jackson turns away and starts out*) Good night.

REUBEN: I'm sorry, Jackson.

## Act Two

*(Jackson doesn't hear, he is off the porch and exiting across stage. The family is quiet for a while. Reuben closes the door)*

EMMETT: Everybody makes mistakes.

RACHEL: That sign is making us crazy!

REUBEN: *(Irritated)* The sign stays up.

*(He hands the bread to Ash and is somewhat distressed as he crosses back into the living room)*

ASH: I think it's too dangerous to keep up now, Reuben. Why not take it down just for tonight? After all, you can always put it back up.

EMMETT: After the funeral wouldn't hurt.

*(Reuben shakes his head "no," the phone rings almost like a reprise. Victor rises to get it)*

REUBEN: Once she's in the ground, they'll forget it.

VICTOR: Hello? Who? *(To Reuben)* It's for you.

REUBEN: *(Continuing)* And if they ever catch the boys, these people won't even remember her name! Besides, it's the principle of the thing. *(Takes phone)* Hello? Who? Sergeant Harrison? No, I'm all right, we're not long back from the layout, so we are a little tired. Unhuh—you caught one of them?

ASH: Thank God!

REUBEN: Unhuh—Well, that's a start. I hope so—*(Smiles suddenly)* You saw the picture in the paper? Yeah, I useta box light-heavy, I was ranked number three for a while. Well, they're supposed to send some people out to interview me. *(Chuckles)* Listen, you open up us bus drivers anything's liable to come out. Unhuh. *(Serious)* There is one thing, though.

53

Could you have a patrol car pass through this street from time to time tonight? No—nothin' serious—fine. Thanks, Sarge. You too! (*Hangs up*) A patrol car will swing through here tonight, are y'all satisfied?

EMMETT: When you ever known the police to be where they're supposed to be, when they're supposed to be there? Man you crazy! I know what I'm-a do, and it ain't gonna wait on no cops eitha!

ASH: (*Giving Emmett a nasty look*) What did he say about the boys?

REUBEN: (*Sitting*) They caught one of 'em—he's fifteen.

ASH: They get younger and weaker in every generation.

REUBEN: (*Disturbed*) There were two of 'em. They picked up some kid named Stockholm and he told on the other one—boy they call Zooman. (*To himself*) I never thought of them as that young—they felt like men.

RACHEL: I'm glad they caught him.

EMMETT: (*Overlapping*) They got 'em out here sellin' dope at ten and eleven—Where have you been, Reub?

REUBEN: You ever heard of them, Victor?

RACHEL: How would Victor know somebody named Zooman?

VICTOR: I've heard of him—I don't know him.

RACHEL: You better not know him!

REUBEN: Is that the one you wanted to get? (*Victor nods*) Did you know he had done it?

VICTOR: Nawww—it was the rumor that it came from down the Bottom and he's the runner down there—(*Shrugs*) So—

RACHEL: What? What kinda crazy—are you in some gang?

VICTOR: No! That was just the rumor on the street—I'm not in no gang! (*A long pause*) Can I sit outside on the steps?

REUBEN: Go 'head. (*Victor rises and starts out*) The kids know who's on the street and who isn't.

RACHEL: (*Calmly*) Will you please take that sign down?

REUBEN: Nope. The cop just said, he thought it was a good idea to leave it up. They got a lotta phone calls today after my picture was in the paper—said a lot of people are behind it.

(*Rachel shakes her head*)

ASH: Rachel, you want an aspirin?

RACHEL: I want this man to take down that damn sign!

REUBEN: Rachel, why can't you back me up! When I was hanging those telephone pole signs? The Democratic Committeeman over on Shelby Street? Man ain't never spoke to me since we moved here—came up to me and told me I was right! Right! Morgan the barber put one in his shop, said it made him feel proud. Cobb at the corner grocery—Baker at the shoeshine parlor, they all said they were for it!

RACHEL: You put up a few signs, get your name in the paper and you're Martin Luther King?

REUBEN: Nobody's trying to be King—If somebody comes forward maybe those boys won't run through here no more!

RACHEL: I thought you put it up for Jinny?

REUBEN: I did!

RACHEL: The people around here want to do something to you, Reuben.

EMMETT: I got to agree with her, Reuben—all that stuff you talkin'—listen, we got to be on guard right here!

REUBEN: Goddamn—don't y'all understand? You can't live across the street from me, see my daughter get killed and not do nothin'! I don't have to be in no newspapers—or TV either! You can't do that shit to me!

RACHEL: You know what they wrote in this book? They want to kill you, Reuben—and I love you!

REUBEN: Then they gonna hafta do it! I'm not scared of them.

RACHEL: You're not scared, but the rest of us are scared to death.

REUBEN: I can't take the sign down, until somebody comes forward—and I don't want anybody in this family to mess with it, eitha!

RACHEL: (*Rising*) We just got through sitting in front of Jinny— and Reuben, I don't want to wind up sitting in front of you. (*Hesitant*) If you don't take it down—I want you to leave!

(*She starts away, and Ash helps her as she starts up the stairs. For a moment there is quiet, then Reuben rises*)

REUBEN: Rachel? I ain't goin' nowhere!

(*Rachel continues as the light fades slowly in the house. Victor rises and starts across the stage toward the platform, which he mounts slowly. He is a little sad*)

VICTOR: They always tell me that I've got a better education than they had—that I know more—should do great things, but they never let me say anything. I don't have a voice in nothin'—no opinions, no pros—cons—and most of the time they talk over me like I'm not even there. And I know a whole lot more than they know. (*Pause*) I'm the one misses Jinny the most—I was around her the most! We useta have arguments sometimes, but she was all I had—you can't talk to them—not like you can with someone you're close to—grow up with. Me and Jinny had secrets—things they never even knew we talked about. They weren't big secrets, but sometimes she would tell me things—like how she wanted them to get back together. And how angry she would get with my Mom when she wouldn't let my father stay here. She told me once that sometimes, when she missed him a lot, she would show off just to get on my Mom's nerves so bad she would have to call my father over, just to punish her. At least she would see him. (*Slight pause*) That's what she was doin' the other day—and they don't know that. I know it, but I'll never tell them!

(*Victor starts off the platform as the light builds slowly across the stage where Zooman enters. Zooman glances at the sign, he notices Victor, who notices him. They both straighten. Zooman reaches into his pocket [the one away from the audience] and removes his knife. We hear it click. He holds it down at his side, out of sight. Victor registers an immediate sense of caution. Both boys are tense as they start toward each other at the same time. They will reach each other and pass in silence, aware and prepared for one another. Victor goes directly to the porch, and looks back at Zooman, who proceeds to the platform, never looking back. When he reaches it, he looks at his knife, closes it and puts it back into his pocket. He smiles as Victor exits through the house. Through all of this, Zooman's music has played*)

ZOOMAN: They got me a little scared. If they got Stockholm's ass in the slams, it's just a matter of time, 'cause the big blues put a lotta pressure on you once they pick you up. Anybody can snap under that. I'm not even sure what *I* would do! 'Specially since I got a previous record—the big blues can be a bitch! At the seventh? They hit my little brother Kenny 'cross the mouth with a blackjack! (*To himself*) Stockholm probably screamed his guts out. Y'all won't have to wait too long—Stock probably gave the Man a complete description by now. I'm not mad with him, though—his Mom probably got him some wise-ass lawyer and that mothafucka will make Stockholm swear he wasn' even there! "Zooman had the gun!" "Zooman fired the shots!" "Zooman told me to do it!" (*Smiles*) It's all right, 'cause I'd put the whole thing on him if I got the chance. Don't *nobody* want to go to jail for murder. My aunt—she'll be down there cryin' all ova the place. My Mom won't come—and my fatha probably won't even know about it, unless they put it in the Chicago papers—(*Shakes head*) That dude—if I had a nickel for every time I laid eyes on that mothafucka I wouldn' have fifty cents! (*Tired*) Last night, I slept squattin' over the toilet seat in the train station with a faggot! Mothafucka had the nerve to proposition me, while I was peein'! I kicked his ass, and when the mothafucka started pleadin' I jes' *cut* the mothafucka—shiiiitt! And y'all got the nerve to hunt me? Y'all let anything walk the streets—and you mothafuckas never showed me no mercy! (*Pause*) I'll be off your streets soon, don't worry—I just got one more thing to do. (*Zooman steps from the platform and starts across the stage boldly toward the Tate house. Before he reaches the steps he is hollering, his knife in his hand*) Hey mothafucka! This is Zooman out here! (*He reaches up and begins to rip and tear at the sign*) Don't nobody do this shit! You don't send people after me! You hear that, mothafucka!? This is Zooman you fuckin' with!

(*Lights come on inside the house and Emmett, half frightened half asleep, emerges from the dining room with a gun in his hand*)

EMMETT: Reuben?

ZOOMAN: (*At once*) Come on out!

(*Emmett fires immediately through the window. The shot hits Zooman and knocks him down, and he pulls down the sign with him. He is in surprised agony for a few moments as he begins to die*)

EMMETT: Reuben! They're outside! Reuben! (*He fires again*) Go 'way!

(*Reuben bursts onto the stage upstairs*)

REUBEN: Emmett—what the hell are you doin'? (*He starts down*)

EMMETT: They're outside! They were pullin' on the sign! I heard 'em—it woke me up! They were tryin' to come in!

(*Reuben starts toward the front door*)

REUBEN: That sounded like some kid—

EMMETT: That wasn' no kid I heard! Them people were comin' in! I heard 'em on the porch! I heard 'em!

(*Rachel and Victor and Ash emerge as Reuben opens the door and steps out onto the porch. Reuben bends over Zooman*)

REUBEN: Be still.

ZOOMAN: I'm Zooman. Fuck you!

(*Zooman dies*)

ASH: (*Overlapping*) What happened, Emmett?

EMMETT: I heard 'em tryin' to get in—they were outside the window, screamin' and yellin'—

(*Rachel is down, and moving toward the door*)

RACHEL: Reuben? Reuben! (*She opens the door*)

EMMETT: (*Dazed, overlapping*) It sounded like they were comin' in—(*Ash moves toward him*) It did to me! (*Emmett drops the pistol as Reuben straightens facing Rachel*)

REUBEN: Call the police—

(*Victor goes to the phone as Rachel steps toward Reuben*)

RACHEL: Who is it, Reuben?

REUBEN: Zooman—

RACHEL: (*Suddenly aware*) Zooman? (*She moves forward menacingly*) This is the one killed my baby? (*To the body*) Get up! (*She is enraged, but Reuben stops her*) I'm-a kill him! Get up goddamnit!

REUBEN: He's dead, Rachel!

(*She struggles to get loose*)

RACHEL: Let him get up!

REUBEN: He's dead!

(*At first she is disbelieving—stunned almost. She seems dazed by the news. But suddenly all the pain and anguish of these awful days builds in her, and she is crying and reaching for Reuben*)

RACHEL: Oh, Reuben—oh my God, Reuben—

(*Reuben puts his arms around her and holds her as she cries*)

REUBEN: I know, baby. I know.

(*Slowly he starts her back toward the house. Reuben and Rachel enter the house as the lights fade out slowly, and another sign slides slowly over the porch. It reads: HERE, LESTER JOHNSON WAS KILLED. HE WILL BE MISSED BY FAMILY AND FRIENDS. HE WAS KNOWN AS ZOOMAN. A spotlight builds to brilliance on this new sign, then slowly fades out. The stage goes to black but Zooman's music lingers in the air, mixed with the sound of a distant siren*)

## THE END